THE **NEW** BOOK OF

Sauces

Other successful titles in this series:

The New Book of
Pasta
ISBN 1 84065 223 3

The New Book of
Cocktails
ISBN 1 84065 225 X

The Book of
Jewish Cooking
ISBN 1 84065 217 9

The Book of
Caribbean Cooking
ISBN 1 84065 061 3

The Book of
Chinese Cooking
ISBN 1 84065 121 0

The Book of
Dips and Salsas
ISBN 1 84065 062 1

The Book of
Finger Food
ISBN 1 84065 063 X

The Book of
Fish & Shellfish Dishes
ISBN 1 84065 129 6

The Book of
Grilling & Barbecues
ISBN 1 84065 270 5

The Book of
Japanese Cooking
ISBN 1 84065 134 2

The Book of
Mediterranean Cooking
ISBN 1 84065 402 3

The Book of
One Pot Cooking
ISBN 1 84065 140 7

The Book of Tapas
& Spanish Cooking
ISBN 1 84065 045 1

The Book of
Thai Cooking
ISBN 1 84065 148 2

The Book of
Wok & Stir Fry Dishes
ISBN 1 84065 403 1

THE NEW BOOK OF
Sauces

ANNE SHEASBY

PHOTOGRAPHED BY
PATRICK McLEAVEY

SALAMANDER

Published by Salamander Books Limited
8 Blenheim Court, Brewery Road, London N7 9NY

9 8 7 6 5 4 3 2 1

© Salamander Books Ltd., 2002

A member of **Chrysalis** Books plc

ISBN 1 84065 224 1

Project managed by: Stella Caldwell
Editor: Madeline Weston
Designer: Sue Storey
Photographer: Patrick McLeavey
Photographer's Assistant: Rebecca Willis
Home Economist: Sandra Miles
Filmset and reproduction by: Studio Tec, England

Printed in Spain

CONTENTS

FOREWORD

Sauces provide the finishing touch to many dishes, enhancing the flavour of food and transforming it into something really special. They are very versatile and can be served with a wide variety of foods and dishes.

The New Book of Sauces is an inspirational collection of tempting recipes suitable for all kinds of foods and for all occasions. We include many basic and classic sauces, as well as flavourful savoury sauces, tempting sweet sauces and coulis, creative salsas and relishes and tasty marinades and pastes.

In this book, you will discover a mouth-watering selection of recipes, both sweet and savoury, all of which combine a whole range of different ingredients that are widely and readily available.

Many of these sauces are quick and simple to make, so, why not try some of these delicious recipes and add that special finishing touch to your own dishes?

INTRODUCTION

Sauces are an essential part of every cook's selection of tried and trusted recipes. A good sauce has the ability to turn something plain or ordinary into something special. A sauce may be thick or thin, smooth or chunky, and a flavourful sweet or savoury sauce can help to create an everyday meal that is both delicious and memorable. The flavour of many basic sauces can also be varied with the addition of one or more ingredients selected from a whole array of foods.

Some sauces are available commercially in various forms including chilled fresh sauces, bottled or canned sauces, or dry packet mixes, which are combined with liquids such as water, stock or milk to make a sauce.

In this book, we include an extensive collection of home-made stocks, basic and classic sauces, sauces ideal for transforming foods such as meat, poultry, fish or vegetables, and sweet sauces, as well as salsas, relishes, marinades and pastes.

At the end of each recipe, we give some serving suggestions, as well as the quantity or number of servings each recipe makes. Some recipes also include additional ideas for ingredient variations to change the flavour of the basic recipe to suit your own tastes.

HOME-MADE STOCKS

Good home-made stocks add a much better flavour to many savoury sauces and it is well worth the small amount of effort it takes to make your own stock. Home-made stocks freeze well and come in handy when you are short of time.

These days, a wide and improved range of stock products is available in

our supermarkets and stores. Ready-made stocks such as chilled fresh stocks are widely available and provide a good alternative, if you don't have time to make your own. Stock cubes or bouillon powder are a further alternative, but they tend to be stronger and more salty in flavour, so should be used sparingly.

TYPES OF SAUCE

A good sauce will complement and enhance the food it is served with and should never overpower the flavour of the dish. Many sauces are simple to make and take a short amount of time, and just a little patience, to create something delicious.

There are several types of sauce including roux-based, brown or emulsified sauces, fruit or vegetable-based sauces, purées or coulis, flavoured butters, sweet sauces for desserts, salsas, relishes, marinades or pastes. Recipes for all these types are included in this book.

ROUX-BASED SAUCES

Roux-based sauces are based on equal quantities of butter and flour that are cooked together. The butter is melted, then the flour is stirred in and this mixture is known as the 'roux'. The roux is cooked for varying lengths of time depending on the recipe, for example, for a classic white sauce the roux is cooked but not coloured, whereas for a brown sauce the roux is cooked for longer until it becomes brown. Liquid is then gradually stirred into the roux and the sauce is then heated, while stirring, until it has thickened.

EMULSIFIED SAUCES

There are two types of emulsified sauce – those based on a butter emulsion (such as hollandaise or béarnaise) or on a cold emulsion of oil and egg yolks (such as mayonnaise or aioli). With emulsified sauces such as hollandaise or beurre blanc, a reduction of the liquid during cooking gives a more intense flavour to the sauce, which is enriched and thickened with the addition of butter or eggs.

FRUIT & VEGETABLE SAUCES & COULIS

Fruit or vegetable-based sauces are very popular and create a whole variety of flavours to accompany a wide range of foods. Fresh fruit coulis are made by simply puréeing and sieving one or more fresh fruits such as raspberries, apricots or mixed berries, to make a pouring sauce. This creates a range of delicious fruit sauces to accompany desserts such as ice cream or yogurt ice, meringues, fresh fruit or fruit tartlets.

SALSAS & RELISHES

Salsas and relishes are a combination of finely chopped ingredients, tossed together with other flavourings, to form a delicious and flavourful sauce. They are simple to make and the ingredients used can be varied a great

deal to create a good range of tempting and interesting flavours.

Salsas and relishes provide a tasty accompaniment to many dishes and are excellent served with barbecued or char-grilled meats, poultry, fish or vegetables.

MARINADES & PASTES

Marinades and pastes are an ideal way of adding flavour to meat, poultry and fish, and occasionally to some vegetables. Marinades or pastes are highly flavoured mixtures of ingredients that heighten the flavour of meat, poultry or fish and often tenderise the meat as well.

Meat, poultry or fish is added to the marinade or paste and turned or brushed to coat it all over. It is then left to soak or stand for 1 hour or more, depending on the recipe.

The food is then removed from the marinade or paste and cooked. Sometimes the marinade may then be used for basting the food during cooking to prevent it from drying out. On occasions the marinade may be reduced or thickened separately to make a sauce, otherwise it is simply discarded. Marinades are particularly good for use when barbecuing or grilling meat and poultry.

THICKENING SAUCES

Sauces may be thickened towards the end of cooking in various ways. Cornflour or arrowroot may be blended with a little water or cold liquid, then added to the sauce and heated, while stirring, until the sauce boils and thickens. Beurre manie (equal quantities of butter and flour are kneaded together then gradually added to hot stock) is another thickener that is added towards the end of the preparation time.

USEFUL EQUIPMENT

Small heavy-based saucepans are ideal to use when making sauces as they ensure slow, even cooking, which is important for many sauces.

A good balloon whisk is a useful tool to have, particularly when making smooth sauces. A whisk will help prevent lumps forming in the sauce as well as ensuring a smooth, even result. If the sauce does not require whisking, a basic wooden spoon is ideal for sauce-making.

When sieving sauces, such as fruit purées to make coulis, a nylon sieve is very helpful. Use a nylon sieve rather than a metal sieve, especially when sieving fruits or acidic foods, as a metal sieve may impart a little metallic

blender or food processor will help to prevent curdling or separation of the ingredients, which can sometimes occur with this type of recipe.

If a roux-based sauce becomes lumpy, simply whisk or beat it briskly until it becomes smooth. If this doesn't work, you can try sieving the sauce or, alternatively, a blender or food processor can be used to process the sauce until smooth.

If an emulsified sauce shows signs of curdling, it may be rescued by adding an ice cube to the sauce and whisking thoroughly until smooth.

To reduce the risk of curdling when making an egg custard sauce or crème Anglaise, add 1 teaspoon cornflour to the egg yolks and sugar. Once the custard has thickened, cook the sauce gently for a little longer to make sure the taste of the cornflour disappears.

If an egg custard sauce shows signs of curdling or separating, strain it into a clean cold bowl, add a few ice cubes and whisk briskly to reduce the temperature of the custard, which should become smooth once again.

flavour or occasionally slight discoloration to the food being sieved, which then may spoil the flavour.

A small blender or food processor can be a useful piece of equipment to have when making some types of sauce. It may simply be used to chop ingredients finely for a sauce or paste, or to purée a sauce to make it smoother and more palatable.

RESCUING LUMPY OR CURDLED SAUCES

When making emulsified sauces such as hollandaise or mayonnaise, a

SERVING SAUCES

Some sauces are best served hot, others are best served cold, while some may be served either way. If serving a thickened sauce cold, such as an egg custard sauce, once it is made, cover the top surface closely with damp greaseproof or non-stick baking paper, to prevent a skin forming as the sauce cools. This also applies to sauces that are made in advance, and are to be reheated later when required.

CHICKEN STOCK

1 meaty chicken carcass
1 onion, sliced
2 carrots, sliced
2 sticks celery, chopped
2 bay leaves
salt and freshly ground black pepper

Break or chop chicken carcass into pieces and place in a large saucepan. Add prepared vegetables, bay leaves, seasoning and 1.7 litres (60fl oz/7½ cups) cold water and stir to mix.

Bring slowly to the boil, reduce the heat, then partially cover the pan and simmer gently for about 2 hours. From time to time, skim off and discard any scum and fat that rises to the surface.

Strain the stock through a fine sieve into a bowl, adjust the seasoning, then set aside to cool quickly. Use immediately, or cover and chill in the refrigerator for up to 3 days. Remove and discard any fat from the surface of the stock and use the stock as required.

Makes about 700ml (25fl oz/3 cups)

VARIATIONS: Use 1 meaty turkey carcass in place of chicken. Use 2 leeks or 6 shallots, in place of onion.

MEAT STOCK

450g (1lb) stewing beef or shoulder of lamb, diced
450g (1lb) beef or lamb bones
6 shallots or 1 large onion, sliced
2 carrots, sliced
1 turnip, chopped
2 sticks celery, sliced
1 fresh bouquet garni
salt and freshly ground black pepper

Preheat the oven to 220C (425F/Gas 7). Put meat and bones in a roasting tin and bake in the oven for about 30 minutes, or until well browned, turning occasionally.

Transfer the meat, bones and juices to a large saucepan and add 1.7 litres (60fl oz/ 7½ cups) cold water. Add the prepared vegetables, bouquet garni and seasoning and stir to mix. Bring slowly to the boil, reduce the heat, then partially cover the pan and simmer gently for about 2 hours. From time to time, skim off and discard any scum and fat that rises to the surface.

Strain the stock through a fine sieve into a bowl, adjust the seasoning, then set aside to cool quickly. Use immediately or cover and chill in the refrigerator for up to 3 days. Remove and discard any fat from the surface of the stock and use the stock as required.

Makes about 700ml (25fl oz/3 cups)

VARIATIONS: Use 115g (4oz) diced swede in place of turnip. Use 1-2 bay leaves in place of bouquet garni. This stock may be frozen in covered container(s) for up to 3 months.

FISH STOCK

1kg (2¼lb) fish bones and trimmings
1 large onion, chopped
1 large carrot, sliced
3 sticks celery, chopped
1 bay leaf
small bunch of fresh parsley
salt and freshly ground black pepper

Wash the fish trimmings and put them in a large saucepan with the prepared vegetables, bay leaf, parsley and seasoning.

Add 1 litre (35fl oz/4½ cups) cold water and stir to mix. Bring slowly to the boil, reduce the heat, then partially cover the pan and simmer gently for about 30 minutes. From time to time, skim off and discard any scum that rises to the surface.

Remove any large bones, then strain the stock through a fine sieve into a bowl, adjust seasoning, and set aside to cool. Use immediately or cover and chill in the refrigerator for up to 2 days. Use as required.

Makes about 850ml (30fl oz/3¾ cups)

VARIATIONS: Use 6 shallots or 2 leeks in place of onion. Use 1 large parsnip, thickly sliced, in place of carrot. This stock may be frozen in covered container(s) for up to 1 month.

VEGETABLE STOCK

1 large onion, chopped
2 leeks, washed and sliced
2 carrots, sliced
4 sticks celery, chopped
175g (6oz) swede, diced
1 parsnip, thickly sliced
1 fresh bouquet garni
8 black peppercorns
½ teaspoon salt

Put all the prepared vegetables, bouquet garni, black peppercorns and salt in a large saucepan. Add 1.7 litres (60fl oz/7½ cups) cold water and stir to mix.

Bring slowly to the boil, reduce the heat, then partially cover the pan and simmer gently for about 1 hour. From time to time, skim off and discard any scum that rises to the surface.

Strain the stock through a fine sieve into a bowl, adjust the seasoning, then set aside to cool. Use immediately or cover and chill in the refrigerator for up to 3 days. Use as required.

Makes about 1.2 litres (40fl oz/5 cups)

VARIATIONS: Use turnip in place of swede. Use 1-2 bay leaves in place of bouquet garni. This stock may be frozen in covered container(s) for up to 3 months.

BASIC WHITE SAUCE

15g (½oz/1 tablespoon) butter
15g (½oz/2 tablespoons) plain flour
300ml (10fl oz/1¼ cups) milk
salt and freshly ground black pepper

Melt the butter in a small saucepan, stir in the flour and cook, stirring, for 1 minute. Remove the pan from the heat and gradually whisk in the milk.

Return to the heat and bring slowly to the boil, stirring or whisking until the sauce is thickened and smooth. Simmer gently for 2 minutes, stirring. Season to taste with salt and pepper. Serve with cooked meat, poultry, fish or vegetables.

Makes about 300ml (10fl oz/1¼ cups)
Serves 4

VARIATION: For a Thick/Coating Sauce, increase the butter to 25g (1oz/2 tablespoons) and flour to 25g (1oz/¼ cup).

FOR A BLENDED WHITE SAUCE
Measure 300ml (10fl oz/1¼ cups) milk. Blend 5 teaspoons cornflour with a little of the milk in a bowl to form a smooth paste. Heat remaining milk in a small saucepan with a knob of butter, until boiling. Pour the hot milk on to the cornflour mixture, stirring continuously. Return the mixture to the saucepan and bring slowly to the boil, stirring, until the sauce thickens. Simmer gently for 2-3 minutes, stirring. Season to taste with salt and pepper. Serve.

— WHITE SAUCE VARIATIONS —

CHEESE (MORNAY) SAUCE

Follow the recipe for Basic White Sauce.
Before seasoning, remove the pan from the
heat and stir in 50g (2oz/½ cup) finely
grated mature Cheddar or Gruyère cheese
and 1 teaspoon Dijon mustard. Add salt and
freshly ground black pepper to taste. Serve
with cooked fish, ham, vegetables or egg
dishes.

PARSLEY SAUCE

Follow the recipe for Basic White Sauce.
Stir in 2-3 tablespoons chopped fresh
parsley just before serving. Serve with
cooked fish, ham, bacon or vegetables.

ONION SAUCE

Finely chop 1 large onion and sauté in 20g
(¾oz/¼ cup) butter for 10-15 minutes, or
until softened. Follow the recipe for Basic
White Sauce. Stir the sautéed onion into
the cooked white sauce just before serving.
Serve with cooked meat, poultry or fish.

BÉCHAMEL SAUCE

300ml (10fl oz/1¼ cups) milk
1 small onion or shallot, cut in half
1 small carrot, thickly sliced
1 bay leaf
6 black peppercorns
a few fresh parsley stalks
15g (½oz/1 tablespoon) butter
15g (½oz/2 tablespoons) plain flour
salt and freshly ground black pepper
freshly grated nutmeg, to taste (optional)

Pour milk into a small saucepan and add onion or shallot, carrot, bay leaf, black peppercorns and parsley stalks.

Bring almost to the boil, then remove the pan from the heat, cover and leave to infuse for 30 minutes. Strain into a jug, reserving the milk and discarding the contents of the sieve. Melt butter in a separate small saucepan, stir in flour and cook, stirring, for 1 minute. Remove the pan from the heat and gradually whisk in infused milk.

Return to the heat and bring slowly to the boil, whisking until the sauce is thickened and smooth. Simmer gently for 2 minutes, stirring. Season with salt and pepper and nutmeg, if using. Serve with fish, grilled chicken or cooked vegetables.

Makes about 300ml (10fl oz/1¼ cups)
Serves 4

VARIATION: For a thicker sauce, increase the butter to 25g (1oz/2 tablespoons) and flour to 25g (1oz/¼ cup).

QUICK TOMATO SAUCE

1 tablespoon olive oil
1 onion, finely chopped
2 cloves garlic, crushed
2 x 400g (14oz) cans chopped tomatoes
2 tablespoons tomato purée
2 tablespoons medium-dry sherry
½ teaspoon caster sugar
salt and freshly ground black pepper

Heat the oil in a saucepan, add onion and garlic and cook gently for 8-10 minutes, stirring occasionally, until softened.

Add the tomatoes with their juice, tomato purée, sherry, sugar and salt and pepper and mix well. Bring to the boil, then cook gently, uncovered, for about 25 minutes, stirring occasionally, until the sauce is thick and pulpy. Adjust the seasoning and serve. Serve with cooked pasta, meat, poultry, fish, vegetables or egg dishes.

Makes about 800ml (28fl oz/3½ cups)
Serves 4-6

VARIATIONS: Stir 1 tablespoon chopped fresh mixed herbs into the sauce just before serving. Use white or red wine in place of sherry.

COOK'S TIP: Once cooked, this sauce may be cooled slightly, then puréed in a blender or food processor until smooth. Reheat gently before serving.

— ESPAGNOLE (BROWN) SAUCE —

25g (1oz/2 tablespoons) butter
1 slice streaky bacon, trimmed and chopped
1 small onion, finely chopped
1 small carrot, finely chopped
1 stick celery, finely chopped
50g (2oz) mushrooms, finely chopped
25g (1oz/¼ cup) plain flour
450ml (16fl oz/2 cups) beef or meat stock
    (see page 13)
2 tablespoons tomato purée
1 fresh bouquet garni
salt and freshly ground black pepper

Melt butter in a saucepan, add the bacon
and cook for 2-3 minutes, stirring.

Add onion, carrot, celery and mushrooms
and cook gently for 6-8 minutes, stirring
occasionally, until softened. Stir in flour and
cook, stirring, until the mixture is brown.
Remove the pan from the heat and
gradually whisk in the stock. Return to the
heat and bring slowly to the boil, stirring or
whisking until the sauce is thickened. Add
the tomato purée, bouquet garni and
seasoning. Partially cover the pan and
simmer gently for about 1 hour, stirring
occasionally.

Strain the sauce into a clean pan and
discard the contents of the sieve. Reheat
gently and adjust the seasoning before
serving. Serve with cooked red meats, game
or offal.

Makes about 300ml (10fl oz/1¼ cups)
Serves 4

VARIATIONS: Use smoked or unsmoked
streaky bacon in this recipe. Smoked bacon
will impart a smoky flavour to the sauce.
Use 2 shallots in place of onion.

RÉMOULADE SAUCE

2 teaspoons capers, drained
3 cocktail gherkins, drained
1 anchovy fillet
150ml (5fl oz/²⁄₃ cup) mayonnaise (see page 30)
1 teaspoon Dijon mustard
2 teaspoons finely chopped fresh tarragon
2 teaspoons chopped fresh parsley
salt and freshly ground black pepper

Finely chop the capers, gherkins and anchovy fillet and place in a bowl.

Add the mayonnaise, mustard, tarragon and parsley and mix well.

Season to taste with salt and pepper. Serve with cooked cold meat and poultry, shellfish and hard-boiled eggs.

Makes about 200ml (7fl oz/scant 1 cup)
Serves 4-6

BEURRE BLANC

3 tablespoons white wine
3 tablespoons white wine vinegar
1 shallot, finely chopped
225g (8oz/1 cup) butter, chilled and cut into small
  cubes
salt and freshly ground black pepper
lemon juice
1 tablespoon chopped fresh parsley (optional)

Put white wine, wine vinegar and shallot in a small saucepan, bring to the boil and boil until reduced to about 2 tablespoons. Strain and return to the pan.

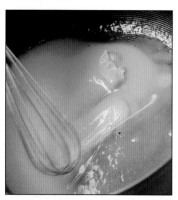

Over a low heat, gradually whisk in the chilled butter, piece by piece. The sauce should become pale, thick and creamy as the butter melts. Remove the pan from the heat to prevent overheating.

Season to taste with salt and pepper and a squeeze of lemon juice. Stir in parsley, if using. Serve with grilled or poached fish or poultry.

Makes about 200ml (7fl oz/scant 1 cup)
Serves 4-6

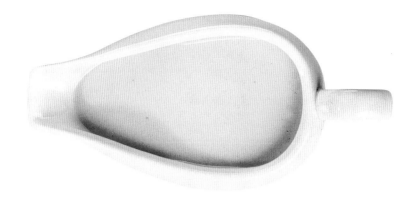

VELOUTÉ SAUCE

20g (¾oz/1½ tablespoons) butter
20g (¾oz/3 tablespoons) plain flour
300ml (10fl oz/1¼ cups) home-made stock (meat,
  chicken, fish or vegetable stock may be used, see
  pages 12-15)
2 tablespoons double cream
½ teaspoon lemon juice
salt and freshly ground black pepper

Melt butter in a small saucepan, stir in flour
and cook, stirring, for about 2 minutes, until
light golden in colour.

Remove the pan from the heat and
gradually whisk in the stock. Return to the
heat and bring slowly to the boil, stirring or
whisking until the sauce is thickened and
smooth. Simmer gently for 2 minutes,
stirring.

Stir in the cream, then stir in the lemon
juice and season to taste with salt and
pepper. Serve with grilled or baked fish,
poultry or meat or cooked vegetables.

Makes about 300ml (10fl oz/1¼ cups)
Serves 4

HOLLANDAISE

3 tablespoons white wine vinegar
6 black peppercorns
1 slice of onion
1 bay leaf
1 blade mace
2 egg yolks
115g (4oz/½ cup) butter, at room temperature, diced
salt and freshly ground black pepper
lemon juice, to taste

Put vinegar in a small saucepan with peppercorns, onion, bay leaf and mace. Bring to the boil and simmer until reduced to 1 tablespoon. Remove from heat; set aside.

Put egg yolks in a heatproof bowl with 15g (½oz/1 tablespoon) of the butter and a pinch of salt and beat together using a balloon whisk. Strain the reduced vinegar into the egg mixture and stir to mix. Place the bowl over a pan of barely simmering water and whisk egg mixture for 3-4 minutes, until pale and beginning to thicken. Gradually whisk in remaining butter, one piece at a time, until mixture begins to thicken and emulsify. Make sure each piece of butter is incorporated into the sauce before adding the next piece.

Remove the bowl from the heat. Whisk for 1 minute. Adjust the seasoning and add lemon juice to taste. Serve immediately with poached fish or shellfish, or cooked vegetables such as asparagus or globe artichokes.

Makes about 150ml (5fl oz/⅔ cup)
Serves 4-6

COOK'S TIP: Hollandaise will curdle if allowed to overheat. If it begins to curdle, add an ice cube and whisk well; the sauce should recombine.

BARBECUE SAUCE

40g (1½oz/3 tablespoons) butter
1 onion, finely chopped
150ml (5fl oz/⅔ cup) tomato juice
2 tablespoons red wine vinegar
1 tablespoon Worcestershire sauce
1 tablespoon light soft brown sugar
2 teaspoons English mustard
1 tablespoon tomato purée
salt and freshly ground black pepper

Melt the butter in a small saucepan, add the onion and cook gently for 8-10 minutes, stirring occasionally, until softened.

Add tomato juice, vinegar, Worcestershire sauce, sugar, mustard, tomato purée and seasoning and mix well. Bring to the boil, then simmer, uncovered, for 10-15 minutes, stirring occasionally.

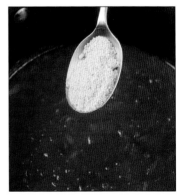

If you would like a smoother sauce, allow the sauce to cool slightly, then purée in a blender or food processor. Reheat gently before serving. Serve with barbecued or grilled meat such as steaks, chops, chicken portions, sausages or burgers.

Makes about 300ml (10fl oz/1¼ cups)
Serves 4-6

VARIATIONS: Use 4 shallots in place of onion. Use passata in place of tomato juice.

FRESH CRANBERRY SAUCE

1 small orange
225g (8oz/2 cups) fresh cranberries
115g (4oz/½ cup) caster or light soft brown sugar
1-2 tablespoons ruby port (optional)

Finely grate the rind from the orange and squeeze the juice.

Place the cranberries in a saucepan with the orange juice, sugar and 150ml (5fl oz/⅔ cup) water. Bring to the boil, then cook gently, uncovered, for 20-30 minutes, stirring occasionally, until the cranberries are soft. Remove the pan from the heat. Using a slotted spoon, remove half the cranberries and place in a bowl. Purée the remaining cranberries and juices in a blender or food processor.

Add the cranberry purée to the reserved cranberries in the bowl, then stir in the orange rind and port, if using, mixing well. Allow to cool, then serve warm or cold with hot or cold roast turkey or pork.

Makes about 300ml (10fl oz/1¼ cups)
Serves 6-8

MINT SAUCE

small bunch of fresh mint, stalks removed
2 teaspoons caster sugar
1 tablespoon boiling water
1 tablespoon white wine vinegar

Wash the mint leaves and shake them dry. Finely chop the mint leaves, then place them in a bowl with the sugar.

Pour on the boiling water, stir to mix, then set aside for 5 minutes, or until the sugar has dissolved.

Add the vinegar and stir to mix. Set aside and leave to stand for 1-2 hours before serving. Serve with roast lamb.

Makes about 3 tablespoons
Serves 4

AIOLI

2 egg yolks
1 tablespoon lemon juice
4 cloves garlic, crushed
½ teaspoon salt
freshly ground black pepper
300ml (10fl oz/1¼ cups) light olive or sunflower oil

Put the egg yolks, lemon juice, garlic, salt, and black pepper to taste in a small blender or food processor and blend for about 20 seconds, until pale and creamy.

With the motor running, gradually add the oil, pouring it in a slow, steady stream through the feeder tube, until the mayonnaise is thick and creamy.

Adjust the seasoning, then use immediately or cover and chill until required. Store in a covered container in the refrigerator for up to 2 days. Serve with cooked cold fish, chicken, meat or shellfish, salads or hard-boiled eggs.

Makes about 300ml (10fl oz/1¼ cups)
Serves 6

VARIATION: Use lime juice in place of lemon juice.

CLASSIC PESTO

50g (2oz) basil leaves
50g (2oz) pine nuts
1 clove garlic, crushed
100ml (3½fl oz/scant ½ cup) olive oil
50g (2oz/½ cup) finely grated fresh Parmesan cheese
salt and freshly ground black pepper

Put the basil leaves, pine nuts, garlic and olive oil in a small blender or food processor and blend to form a fairly smooth paste.

Add the Parmesan and salt and pepper and process briefly to mix. Store in a covered jar in the refrigerator for up to 1 week. Serve with pasta, grilled chicken or poached fish.

Makes about 250ml (9fl oz/generous 1 cup)
Serves 4-6

COOK'S TIP: Alternatively, place basil, pine nuts and garlic in a mortar with a little oil and pound together. Gradually work in remaining oil, then stir in cheese and seasoning.

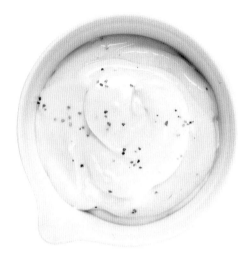

MAYONNAISE

2 egg yolks
1 teaspoon Dijon mustard
1 tablespoon lemon juice or white wine vinegar
pinch caster sugar
½ teaspoon salt
freshly ground black pepper
300ml (10fl oz/1¼ cups) light olive or sunflower oil

Put the egg yolks, mustard, lemon juice or vinegar, sugar, salt, and black pepper to taste in a small blender or food processor.

Blend for about 20 seconds, until smooth, pale and creamy.

With the motor running, gradually add the oil, pouring it in a slow, steady stream through the feeder tube, until the mayonnaise is thick, creamy and smooth. Adjust the seasoning, then use immediately or cover and chill until required. Store in a covered container in the refrigerator for up to 3 days. Serve with salads, cooked cold meats, smoked fish and other cold savoury foods.

Makes about 300ml (10fl oz/1¼ cups)
Serves 6

— MAYONNAISE VARIATIONS —

FLAVOUR VARIATIONS: For Lemon Mayonnaise, use lemon juice and stir 1½ teaspoons finely grated lemon rind into mayonnaise, just before serving.

For Garlic & Herb Mayonnaise, add 1 crushed clove garlic with the egg yolks. Fold 2 tablespoons chopped fresh mixed herbs (such as chives, parsley, tarragon and oregano) into mayonnaise just before serving.

For Horseradish Mayonnaise, fold 2 tablespoons hot horseradish sauce into mayonnaise, just before serving.

For Mustard Mayonnaise, fold 2 tablespoons Dijon or grainy mustard into mayonnaise, just before serving.

For Curried Mayonnaise, fold 1-2 tablespoons curry paste into mayonnaise, just before serving.

TRADITIONAL GRAVY

25g (1oz/2 tablespoons) butter
15g (½oz/2 tablespoons) plain flour
2 shallots, chopped
300ml (10fl oz/1¼ cups) chicken or meat stock (see
   pages 12-13) or water from cooking vegetables
1 teaspoon yeast extract
1 teaspoon dried mixed herbs
salt and freshly ground black pepper

Put 15g (½oz/1 tablespoon) of the butter and all the flour in a small bowl and mix together until well blended to make beurre manie. Set aside.

Melt the remaining butter in a small saucepan, add the shallots and cook gently for 8-10 minutes, stirring occasionally, until softened. Stir in the stock or vegetable water, yeast extract and herbs and bring to the boil. Reduce the heat, cover and simmer for 5 minutes. Remove the shallots using a slotted spoon and discard them. Bring the liquid back to the boil, then add the beurre manie a little at a time, whisking continuously to blend in well with the liquid, until all the beurre manie has been added.

Continue to cook, whisking, until the gravy thickens. Simmer gently for 5 minutes, stirring. Season to taste. Serve with roast meats such as beef, lamb, pork or chicken. (Add any juices from the roasted meat to the gravy for extra flavour and colour.)

Makes about 175ml (6fl oz/¾ cup)
Serves 2-4

VARIATION: Replace 50ml (2fl oz/ ¼ cup) of the stock with red or white wine, if liked.

BLUE CHEESE SAUCE

15g (½oz/1 tablespoon) butter
2 shallots, finely chopped
1 stick celery, finely chopped
2 tablespoons dry sherry
200ml (7fl oz/scant 1 cup) crème fraiche
85g (3oz) blue cheese such as Stilton
  or Gorgonzola, crumbled
1 tablespoon chopped fresh parsley
salt and freshly ground black pepper

Melt the butter in a small saucepan, add the shallots and celery and cook gently for 10-15 minutes, stirring occasionally, until softened.

Add the sherry and boil until reduced slightly. Add the crème fraiche, bring to the boil and bubble for about 5 minutes, stirring occasionally, until thickened slightly.

Stir in the blue cheese until melted, then stir in the parsley. Add salt and pepper to taste. Serve with grilled or barbecued meat or poultry such as steaks or chicken portions. This sauce is also good served with cooked vegetables.

Makes about 325ml (11fl oz/1⅓ cups)
Serves 4

VARIATIONS: Use 1 small onion in place of shallots. Use fresh chives in place of parsley.

HORSERADISH CREAM

150ml (5fl oz/⅔ cup) double cream
2-3 tablespoons grated fresh horseradish
   (depending on taste)
2 teaspoons white wine vinegar
salt and freshly ground black pepper
caster sugar, to taste

Pour the cream into a bowl and whip until thick.

In a separate bowl, mix the horseradish and vinegar together.

Fold into the whipped cream, then add salt, pepper and sugar to taste. Cover and chill in the refrigerator until ready to serve. Serve with hot or cold roast beef. This sauce is also good served with cooked fresh or smoked mackerel or smoked salmon or trout.

Makes about 250ml (9fl oz/1 cup)
Serves 4-6

—— WILD MUSHROOM SAUCE ——

2 tablespoons olive oil
3 shallots, finely chopped
2 cloves garlic, crushed
225g (8oz) fresh mixed wild mushrooms such as
  shiitake and oyster mushrooms, sliced
115g (4oz) chestnut mushrooms, sliced
175ml (6fl oz/¾ cup) dry white wine
85ml (3fl oz/⅓ cup) hot vegetable stock (see page 15)
200ml (7fl oz/scant 1 cup) crème fraîche
salt and freshly ground black pepper
2 tablespoons chopped fresh flat-leaf parsley

Heat oil in a saucepan, add shallots and garlic and cook gently for 8-10 minutes, stirring occasionally, until softened.

Add all the mushrooms and cook for 3-4 minutes, stirring occasionally, until tender. Add the wine, bring to the boil and bubble until reduced by about half. Add the stock, crème fraîche and salt and pepper, bring to the boil and bubble for about 5 minutes or until the sauce thickens slightly, stirring occasionally.

Stir in the parsley and serve with grilled, roast or pan-fried meats and poultry such as steaks, chops or chicken or turkey portions.

Makes about 700ml (25fl oz/3 cups)
Serves 6

VARIATIONS: Use 1 onion in place of the shallots. Use button or closed cup mushrooms in place of chestnut mushrooms.

LEMON CAPER SAUCE

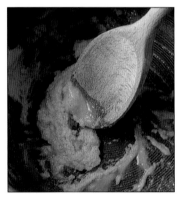

25g (1oz) butter
25g (1oz) plain flour
300ml (10fl oz/1¼ cups) milk
2 tablespoons capers, drained and chopped
1 tablespoon vinegar from jar of capers
finely grated rind of 1 small lemon
salt and freshly ground black pepper

Melt the butter in a small saucepan, stir in the flour and cook, stirring, for 1 minute. Remove the pan from the heat and gradually whisk in the milk.

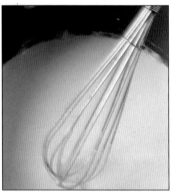

Return to the heat and bring slowly to the boil, stirring or whisking until the sauce is thickened and smooth. Simmer gently for 2 minutes, stirring.

Stir in the capers, vinegar and lemon rind and reheat gently until almost boiling. Season to taste with salt and pepper. Serve with roast or grilled meat such as lamb, pork or ham. This sauce is also good served with poached or grilled white fish.

Makes about 350ml (12fl oz/1½ cups)
Serves 4

– RED WINE (BURGUNDY) SAUCE –

25g (1oz) butter
1 small onion, finely chopped
1 clove garlic, crushed
2 tablespoons plain flour
2 teaspoons light soft brown sugar
300ml (10fl oz/1¼ cups) burgundy or red wine
1 tablespoon medium-dry sherry
1 teaspoon chopped fresh thyme
salt and freshly ground black pepper

Melt the butter in a small saucepan, add onion and garlic and cook for 8-10 minutes, stirring, until softened. Stir in flour and sugar and cook for 1 minute, stirring.

Remove the pan from the heat and gradually whisk in the wine and sherry. Return to the heat and bring slowly to the boil, stirring or whisking continuously, until the sauce is thickened. Simmer gently for 2 minutes, stirring.

Stir in the thyme and season to taste with salt and pepper. Serve, or, if liked, cool slightly, then purée in a blender or food processor until smooth. Reheat gently before serving. Serve with grilled or pan-fried meat such as steak or lamb.

Makes about 300ml (10fl oz/1¼ cups)
Serves 4-6

VARIATIONS: Use 2 shallots in place of onion. Use chopped fresh rosemary or oregano in place of thyme.

— CREAMY ARTICHOKE SAUCE —

40g (1½ oz) butter
3 shallots, finely chopped
25g (1oz) plain flour
300ml (10fl oz/1¼ cups) vegetable stock
  (see page 15)
150ml (5fl oz/⅔ cup) double cream
400g (14oz) can artichoke hearts,
  drained and chopped
salt and freshly ground black pepper

Melt the butter in a saucepan, add the shallots and sauté for 6-8 minutes, until softened. Stir in the flour and cook gently for 1 minute, stirring.

Remove the pan from the heat and gradually whisk in the stock, then stir in the cream. Return to the heat and bring slowly to the boil, stirring or whisking continuously, until the sauce is thickened. Simmer gently for 2 minutes, stirring.

Stir in the artichoke hearts, then reheat gently until hot, stirring. Season to taste with salt and pepper. Serve with grilled or baked chicken or turkey portions. This sauce is also good served with grilled or baked white or oily fish.

Makes about 700ml (25fl oz/3 cups)
Serves 4-6

VARIATIONS: Use 1 small leek in place of shallots. Use milk in place of vegetable stock.

PEANUT SATAY SAUCE

115g (4oz) dry roasted peanuts
1 tablespoon olive oil
1 onion, finely chopped
2 cloves garlic, crushed
1 fresh red chilli, cored, seeded and finely chopped
2.5cm (1in) piece fresh root ginger,
  peeled and finely chopped
400g (14oz) can coconut milk
juice of 1 lime
1 tablespoon light soft brown sugar
salt, to taste

Put the peanuts in a blender or food processor and process until they are finely chopped. Set aside.

Heat the oil in a saucepan, add the onion and sauté for 5 minutes, until softened. Add the garlic, chilli and ginger and cook for 2 minutes, stirring. Add the onion mixture to the peanuts in the processor and process briefly to mix.

Transfer the mixture to the saucepan, add the coconut milk, lime juice and sugar and mix well. Bring slowly to the boil, then reduce the heat and simmer, uncovered, for 10-15 minutes, or until the sauce is thickened, stirring occasionally. Season to taste with salt, if required. Serve as a dipping sauce with grilled or barbecued chicken, beef, lamb or pork kebabs or grilled chicken or turkey portions.

Makes about 500ml (18fl oz/2¼ cups)
Serves 6-8

TARRAGON SAUCE

20g (¾ oz) butter
20g (¾ oz) plain flour
150ml (5fl oz/⅔ cup) vegetable stock
  (see page 15)
150ml (5fl oz/⅔ cup) milk
4 tablespoons double cream
1½ teaspoons French mustard
1 tablespoon chopped fresh tarragon
salt and freshly ground black pepper

Melt the butter in a small saucepan, stir in the flour and cook, stirring, for 1 minute. Remove the pan from the heat and gradually whisk in the stock, milk and cream.

Return to the heat and bring slowly to the boil, stirring or whisking until the sauce is thickened and smooth. Simmer gently for 2 minutes, stirring.

Stir in the mustard and tarragon and season to taste with salt and pepper. Serve with grilled or barbecued poultry or meat such as chicken breasts or lamb cutlets. This sauce is also good served with grilled, baked or pan-fried white fish.

Makes about 350ml (12fl oz/1½ cups)
Serves 4

VARIATION: Stir 50g (2oz) finely grated Cheddar cheese into sauce, just before serving, if liked.

PLUM & GINGER SAUCE

1 tablespoon sunflower oil
2 shallots, finely chopped
1 clove garlic, crushed
2 teaspoons grated fresh root ginger
350g (12oz) red dessert plums, halved,
  pitted and chopped
150ml (5fl oz/⅔ cup) red wine
25g (1oz) light soft brown sugar
1 tablespoon brandy (optional)

Heat the oil in a saucepan, add the shallots, garlic and ginger and cook gently for 5 minutes, stirring occasionally. Add the plums and sauté for 1 minute, stirring.

Stir in the wine and sugar and heat gently, stirring, until the sugar has dissolved. Bring slowly to the boil, then reduce the heat, cover and simmer for about 10 minutes, or until the plums are soft.

Remove the pan from the heat and cool slightly, then purée the mixture in a blender or food processor until smooth. Return the sauce to the rinsed-out pan and stir in the brandy, if using. Reheat gently until hot. Serve hot or cold with roast or barbecued meat such as beef, pork, lamb or duck.

Makes about 425ml (15fl oz/2 cups)
Serves 6-8

GREEN PEPPERCORN SAUCE

150ml (5fl oz/⅔ cup) dry white wine
2 tablespoons brandy
200ml (7fl oz/scant 1 cup) crème fraîche
1 teaspoon Dijon mustard
1 tablespoon green peppercorns in brine,
  rinsed and drained
2 tablespoons chopped fresh parsley
salt and freshly ground black pepper

Put the wine and brandy in a small saucepan and bring to the boil. Simmer, uncovered, for about 10 minutes or until the liquid has reduced by about half.

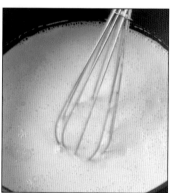

Whisk the crème fraîche into the sauce, bring slowly to the boil, then bubble for about 10 minutes, or until the sauce is thickened slightly.

Whisk the mustard into the sauce, then stir in the green peppercorns and parsley. Season to taste with salt and pepper. Serve with grilled or pan-fried meat or poultry such as beef, pork, duck or chicken. This sauce is also good served with grilled or pan-fried white or oily fish.

Makes about 200ml (7fl oz/1 cup)
Serves 2-4

— SPICY THAI DIPPING SAUCE —

3 spring onions
2 tablespoons light soy sauce
3 tablespoons lemon juice
2 tablespoons medium chilli sauce
½ teaspoon Thai 7-spice seasoning
1 tablespoon chopped fresh coriander
1-2 teaspoons light soft brown sugar

Finely chop the spring onions.

Place the spring onions in a small bowl with the soy sauce, lemon juice, chilli sauce and Thai seasoning and mix well.

Stir in the chopped coriander. Stir in the sugar to taste. Serve as a dipping sauce with cooked Thai beef, pork or chicken dishes.

Makes about 150ml (5fl oz/⅔ cup)
Serves 4

VARIATIONS: Use lime juice in place of lemon juice. Use fish sauce in place of chilli sauce.

TOMATO & BASIL SAUCE

700g (1½lb) fresh plum tomatoes
1 tablespoon olive oil
1 red onion, finely chopped
2 cloves garlic, crushed
2 sticks celery, finely chopped
4 sun-dried tomatoes in oil, drained and
   finely chopped
6 tablespoons red wine
1 tablespoon tomato purée
½ teaspoon caster sugar
salt and freshly ground black pepper
3-4 tablespoons chopped fresh basil

Using a sharp knife, cut a small cross in base of each tomato.

Place the tomatoes in a bowl, cover with boiling water; leave for 30 seconds. Remove using a slotted spoon and plunge into cold water, then drain well. Peel off skins, then halve tomatoes and remove and discard the seeds. Chop flesh and set aside. Heat oil in a saucepan, add onion, garlic and celery and cook gently for 5 minutes, stirring occasionally. Add chopped tomatoes, sun-dried tomatoes, red wine, tomato purée, sugar and seasoning and mix well. Bring to the boil, then reduce the heat, cover and simmer for 15 minutes, stirring occasionally.

Uncover the pan, increase the heat slightly and cook for a further 10-15 minutes, stirring occasionally, until the mixture is thick and pulpy. Stir in the chopped basil and adjust the seasoning to taste. Serve with grilled, baked or pan-fried white fish such as monkfish, haddock or mackerel. This sauce is also good served with cooked hot pasta.

Makes about 700ml (25fl oz/3 cups)
Serves 4-6

WATERCRESS SAUCE

1 bunch of watercress (about 100g/3½oz
 total weight)
25g (1oz/2 tablespoons) butter
25g (1oz/¼ cup) plain flour
300ml (10fl oz/1¼ cups) fish or vegetable stock
 (see pages 14-15)
150ml (5fl oz/⅔ cup) double cream
salt and freshly ground black pepper

Trim the watercress, then blanch it in
boiling water for 30 seconds. Refresh under
cold running water, drain well and pat dry
with absorbent paper towels. Chop finely,
then set aside.

Melt the butter in a small saucepan, then stir
in the flour and cook gently for 1 minute,
stirring. Remove the pan from the heat and
gradually whisk in the stock and cream.
Return to the heat and bring slowly to the
boil, stirring or whisking continuously, until
the sauce is thickened and smooth. Simmer
gently for 2 minutes, stirring.

Add the watercress and cook gently for
1 minute, stirring. Season to taste. If you
like, allow to cool slightly, then purée in a
blender or food processor. Reheat gently.
Serve with grilled or baked fish such as
salmon or tuna steaks or trout or mackerel
fillets. This sauce is also good served with
grilled or baked chicken or turkey.

Makes about 500ml (18fl oz/2¼ cups)
Serves 4-6

VARIATION: Use milk in place of stock.

— CREAMY MUSHROOM SAUCE —

150ml (5fl oz/⅔ cup) fish or vegetable stock
  (see pages 14-15)
300ml (10fl oz/1¼ cups) double cream
40g (1½oz/3 tablespoons) butter
175g (6oz) chestnut mushrooms, sliced
115g (4oz) button mushrooms, sliced
1-2 tablespoons chopped fresh mixed herbs such as
  parsley, chives and tarragon or coriander
salt and freshly ground black pepper

Pour the stock and cream into a saucepan. Bring slowly to the boil, then simmer gently until the sauce thickens slightly to a coating consistency, stirring frequently.

Meanwhile, melt the butter in a frying pan, add all the mushrooms and sauté for about 5 minutes, until soft. Increase the heat slightly and cook, stirring frequently, until all the liquid has evaporated.

Add the mushrooms and chopped herbs to the cream sauce and reheat gently, stirring. Season to taste with salt and pepper. Serve with grilled, baked or poached fish such as cod, monkfish or salmon. This sauce is also good served with grilled meats or poultry.

Makes about 600ml (21fl oz/2¾ cups)
Serves 4-6

VARIATIONS: Use closed cup mushrooms in place of chestnut mushrooms and fresh wild mushrooms in place of button mushrooms.

——— DILL & MUSTARD SAUCE ———

200ml (7fl oz/scant 1 cup) dry white wine
200ml (7fl oz/scant 1 cup) fish or vegetable stock
  (see pages 14-15)
200ml (7fl oz/scant 1 cup) crème fraîche
2 tablespoons wholegrain mustard
2 egg yolks
2 tablespoons chopped fresh dill
salt and freshly ground black pepper

Put the wine and stock in a saucepan, bring
to the boil and boil until reduced by half.

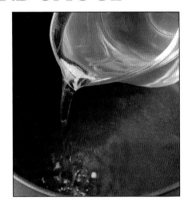

Reduce the heat and stir in the crème
fraîche, mustard, egg yolks and dill. Cook
gently, stirring continuously, for about
10 minutes, or until the sauce is thickened
slightly. Do not allow the mixture to boil.

Season to taste with salt and pepper. Serve
with pan-fried or grilled fish such as plaice,
halibut, haddock or mackerel.

Makes about 400ml (14fl oz/1¾ cups)
Serves 6

VARIATIONS: Use 2-3 teaspoons hot
horseradish sauce or to taste, in place of dill.
Use double cream in place of crème fraîche.

AVOCADO SAUCE

1 lime or 1 small lemon
2 ripe avocados
200ml (7fl oz/scant 1 cup) plain yogurt
100ml (3½fl oz/scant ½ cup) mayonnaise
  (see page 30)
1 tablespoon chopped fresh chives
salt and freshly ground black pepper

Finely grate the rind and squeeze the juice from the lime.

Peel, halve and stone the avocados, then roughly chop the flesh. Place the avocado flesh and lime rind and juice in a blender or food processor.

Add the yogurt and mayonnaise and blend until smooth and well mixed. Add the chives and blend briefly to mix. Season to taste with salt and pepper. Serve immediately with grilled or baked fish such as salmon, tuna or trout, stir-fried tiger prawns or cold cooked seafood such as prawns.

Makes about 600ml (21fl oz/2¾ cups)
Serves 6-8

VARIATION: Use parsley in place of chives.

WHITE WINE SAUCE

175ml (6fl oz/¾ cup) dry white wine
200ml (7fl oz/scant 1 cup) double cream
100ml (3½fl oz/scant ½ cup) fish or vegetable stock
  (see pages 14-15)
1 tablespoon chopped fresh dill (optional)
1 tablespoon chopped fresh parsley
salt and freshly ground black peppe

Pour the wine into a small saucepan, bring to the boil, then boil rapidly until reduced by half.

Stir in the cream and stock, bring to the boil and simmer for 10-15 minutes, stirring occasionally, until the sauce has thickened slightly.

Remove the pan from the heat and stir in the chopped dill, if using, and chopped parsley. Season to taste with salt and pepper. Serve with grilled, baked or poached white fish such as plaice, halibut or lemon sole. This sauce is also good served with grilled or pan-fried chicken or turkey.

Makes about 300ml (10fl oz/1¼ cups)
Serves 4-6

VARIATION: Use crème fraîche in place of double cream.

CREAMY CRAB SAUCE

20g (¾ oz/1½ tablespoons) butter
20g (¾ oz/3 tablespoons) plain flour
150ml (5fl oz/⅔ cup) milk
150ml (5fl oz/⅔ cup) fish or vegetable stock
  (see pages 14-15)
100ml (3½fl oz/scant ½ cup) double cream
225g (8oz) cooked crabmeat, flaked
2 tablespoons chopped fresh coriander
salt and freshly ground black pepper

Melt the butter in a small saucepan, then stir in the flour and cook gently for 1 minute, stirring.

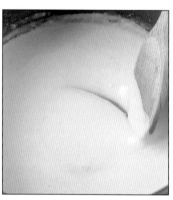

Remove the pan from the heat and gradually whisk in the milk, stock and cream. Return to the heat and bring slowly to the boil, stirring or whisking continuously, until the sauce is thickened and smooth. Simmer gently for 2 minutes, stirring.

Stir in the crabmeat and reheat gently until hot. Stir in the chopped coriander and season to taste with salt and pepper. Serve hot with poached or baked white fish such as cod, haddock or monkfish.

Makes about 600ml (21fl oz/2¾ cups)
Serves 4-6

VARIATIONS: Use two 170g (6oz) cans white crabmeat in brine, drained and flaked, if fresh crabmeat is not available. Use chopped fresh parsley or chives in place of coriander.

— PEPPERED PARSLEY SAUCE —

50g (2oz) fresh flat-leaf parsley
25g (1oz/2 tablespoons) pine nuts
1 clove garlic, crushed
25g (1oz/¼ cup) finely grated fresh Parmesan cheese
½ teaspoon cayenne pepper
½ teaspoon freshly ground black pepper
6 tablespoons olive oil
salt
squeeze of lemon juice (optional)

Put parsley, pine nuts, garlic, Parmesan, cayenne, black pepper and 1 tablespoon of the oil in a small blender or food processor and blend to form a fairly smooth paste.

With the motor running, gradually add the remaining oil pouring it in a steady stream through the feeder tube, until it is well incorporated.

Season to taste with salt and a squeeze of lemon juice, if liked. Add extra cayenne or black pepper, to taste, if liked. Serve with grilled or baked fish such as cod, salmon or monkfish.

Makes about 200ml (7fl oz/scant 1 cup)
Serves 4-6

VARIATIONS: Use fresh basil in place of parsley. Use blanched almonds in place of pine nuts.

— SEAFOOD COCKTAIL SAUCE —

200ml (7fl oz/scant 1 cup) mayonnaise (see page 30)
4 tablespoons extra-thick double cream
2 tablespoons tomato ketchup
1 teaspoon Worcestershire sauce
1 teaspoon lemon juice
few drops of Tabasco sauce
salt and freshly ground black pepper

Put the mayonnaise and cream in a bowl and beat together until smooth and well mixed.

Add the tomato ketchup, Worcestershire sauce, lemon juice and Tabasco and mix well.

Season to taste with salt and pepper. Serve with cooked cold seafood such as prawns, scallops or flaked crabmeat.

Makes about 350ml (12fl oz/1½ cups)
Serves 4-6

VARIATIONS: Use lime juice in place of lemon juice. Add 2 teaspoons creamed horseradish sauce with the Tabasco sauce, if liked.

TARTARE SAUCE

50g (2oz) gherkins, drained
2 tablespoons capers, drained
250ml (9fl oz/generous 1 cup) mayonnaise
  (see page 30)
4 tablespoons extra-thick double cream
1 tablespoon tarragon vinegar
1 tablespoon chopped fresh flat-leaf parsley
1 tablespoon chopped fresh chives
2 teaspoons chopped fresh tarragon
salt and freshly ground black pepper

Finely chop the gherkins and capers and place in a bowl.

Add the mayonnaise and mix well, then fold in the cream.

Stir in the vinegar and chopped herbs, mixing well. Season to taste with salt and pepper. Cover and leave in a cool place for about 30 minutes before serving, to allow the flavours to develop. Serve with grilled, baked or poached fish such as cod or haddock.

Makes about 400ml (14fl oz/1¾ cups)
Serves 8-10

VARIATION: Use white wine vinegar or lemon juice in place of tarragon vinegar.

—— PARSLEY & LEMON SAUCE ——

300ml (10fl oz/1¼ cups) milk
1 shallot, cut in half
1 bay leaf
1 blade of mace
6 black peppercorns
20g (¾oz/1½ tablespoons) butter
20g (¾oz/3 tablespoons) plain flour
100ml (3½fl oz/scant ½ cup) double cream
2 egg yolks
finely grated rind of 1 small lemon
3 tablespoons chopped fresh flat-leaf parsley
salt and freshly ground black pepper

Pour milk into a saucepan and add shallot, bay leaf, mace blade and peppercorns.

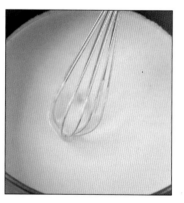

Bring almost to the boil, then remove the pan from the heat, cover and leave to infuse for 30 minutes. Strain into a jug, reserving the milk and discarding the contents of the sieve. Put the butter in a small saucepan with the flour, cream and infused milk. Heat gently, whisking continuously, until the sauce comes to the boil and is thickened and smooth. Simmer gently for 3-4 minutes, stirring. Remove the pan from the heat and gently whisk in the egg yolks.

Stir in the lemon rind and chopped parsley. Return to the heat and cook gently for 1-2 minutes longer, stirring all the time. Do not allow the sauce to boil. Season to taste with salt and pepper. Serve with cooked vegetables such as globe or Jerusalem artichokes, asparagus, green beans or broad beans. This sauce is also good served with grilled fish.

Makes about 400ml (14fl oz/1¾ cups)
Serves 4-6

CREAMED CURRY SAUCE

40g (1½oz/3 tablespoons) butter
4 shallots, finely chopped
1 clove garlic, crushed
2 tablespoons plain flour
3 tablespoons medium-hot curry paste
1 tablespoon tomato purée
300ml (10fl oz/1¼ cups) vegetable stock
  (see page 15)
150ml (5fl oz/⅔ cup) single cream
salt and freshly ground black pepper (optional)

Melt the butter in a small saucepan, add the shallots and cook gently for 8-10 minutes, stirring occasionally, until softened and lightly browned.

Add the garlic and cook for 1 minute. Add the flour and cook for 1 minute, stirring, then add the curry paste and tomato purée. Remove the pan from the heat and gradually whisk in the stock. Bring to the boil, whisking or stirring continuously, until the sauce thickens. Simmer gently for 2 minutes, stirring.

Add the cream and reheat gently until hot, stirring, but do not boil. Add salt and pepper to taste, if required. Serve with cooked vegetables such as cauliflower florets, green beans or okra. This sauce is also good served with grilled or pan-fried chicken or turkey or smoked haddock.

Makes about 550ml (20fl oz/2½ cups)
Serves 4-6

VARIATION: Use 1 onion in place of shallots.

HERBY YOGURT SAUCE

200ml (7fl oz/scant 1 cup) Greek yogurt
100ml (3½fl oz/scant ½ cup) plain yogurt
1 clove garlic, crushed
finely grated rind of 1 lime (optional)
2 tablespoons chopped fresh mixed herbs,
   such as parsley, chives, oregano and mint
salt and freshly ground black pepper

Put the Greek yogurt and plain yogurt in a bowl and fold together to mix.

Add the garlic, lime rind, if using, and chopped herbs and stir to mix well.

Season to taste with salt and pepper. Serve immediately with raw vegetables such as cherry tomatoes, carrots or a mixed salad, or serve with lightly cooked cold vegetables such as green beans.

Makes about 325ml (11fl oz/1⅓ cups)
Serves 4-6

VARIATIONS: Use 1-2 tablespoons chopped fresh mint in place of mixed herbs. Use finely grated rind of 1 small lemon in place of lime rind.

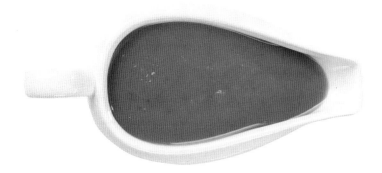

GRILLED PEPPER SAUCE

4 red peppers
1 tablespoon olive oil
1 small red onion, finely chopped
1 stick celery, finely chopped
1 clove garlic, crushed
150ml (5fl oz/⅔ cup) tomato juice
100ml (3½fl oz/scant ½ cup) vegetable stock
   (see page 15)
salt and freshly ground black pepper

Preheat the grill to high. Cut peppers in half and place them cut-side down on the rack in a grill pan. Grill for 10-15 minutes until skin is blackened and charred.

Remove from the grill and cover peppers with a clean damp tea towel. Set aside to cool. Once cool, remove skin, cores and seeds and cut the flesh into chunks. Set aside. Heat the oil in a saucepan, add the onion and celery and cook gently for 8-10 minutes, stirring occasionally, until softened. Add the pepper flesh and garlic and cook for 1-2 minutes, stirring. Add the tomato juice, stock and salt and pepper and mix well. Bring to the boil, then reduce the heat, cover and cook gently for 15-20 minutes, stirring occasionally.

Remove pan from the heat, cool slightly, then purée mixture in a blender or food processor until smooth. Push purée through a sieve and discard contents of sieve. Reheat sauce gently or cool and chill before serving. Adjust seasoning to taste. Serve with cooked vegetables such as broccoli, cauliflower or courgettes or with a vegetable terrine. This sauce is also good served with grilled or baked chicken portions.

Makes about 400ml (14fl oz/1¾ cups)
Serves 4-6

— SPINACH & NUTMEG SAUCE —

225g (8oz) fresh spinach leaves
25g (1oz/2 tablespoons) butter
3 shallots, finely chopped
1 clove garlic, crushed
100ml (3½fl oz/scant ½ cup) vegetable stock
  (see page 15)
2 bay leaves
1 sprig of thyme
4 tablespoons crème fraiche
½ teaspoon freshly grated nutmeg, or to taste
salt and freshly ground black pepper

Wash spinach thoroughly, shake dry, then remove and discard any tough stalks. Chop spinach roughly, then set aside.

Melt the butter in a saucepan, add shallots and sauté for 5 minutes, stirring occasionally. Add garlic and sauté for 1 minute. Add spinach, stock, bay leaves and sprig of thyme. Bring to the boil, then reduce the heat, cover and cook gently for 10 minutes, stirring occasionally. Remove the pan from the heat and allow to cool slightly. Remove and discard bay leaves and thyme. Purée the mixture in a blender or food processor until smooth.

Return to the rinsed-out pan and stir in the crème fraiche. Reheat gently until hot, stirring. Season to taste with nutmeg, salt and pepper. Serve with cooked vegetables such as carrots, baby sweetcorn or new potatoes. This sauce is also good served with grilled or baked fish or chicken.

Makes about 450ml (16fl oz/2 cups)
Serves 6

VARIATION: Use ground cumin in place of nutmeg.

TOMATO & CHILLI SAUCE

40g (1½oz/3 tablespoons) butter
1 leek, washed and finely chopped
1 small red pepper, seeded and finely chopped
1 clove garlic, crushed
2 fresh red chillies, cored, seeded and finely chopped
1½ teaspoons ground cumin
1½ teaspoons ground coriander
400g (14oz) can chopped tomatoes
150ml (5fl oz/⅔ cup) dry white wine
2 tablespoons tomato purée
salt and freshly ground black pepper

Melt butter in a saucepan, add leek, red pepper, garlic and chillies and cook gently for 8-10 minutes, stirring, until softened.

Add ground spices and cook for 1 minute, stirring. Add chopped tomatoes with their juice, wine, tomato purée and salt and pepper and stir to mix. Bring to the boil, then reduce the heat, cover and simmer for 10 minutes, stirring occasionally.

Uncover the pan, increase the heat and cook for a further 10-15 minutes, stirring occasionally, until the sauce has thickened. Check and adjust the seasoning. Serve with cooked or roast vegetables such as parsnips, Brussels sprouts or courgettes. This sauce is also good served with hot pasta.

Makes about 700ml (25fl oz/3 cups)
Serves 6

VARIATION: Use red wine or vegetable stock in place of white wine.

LEMON BUTTER

115g (4oz/½ cup) unsalted butter at room
 temperature
finely grated rind of 1 lemon
2 teaspoons fresh lemon juice
freshly ground black pepper

Place butter in a bowl and beat until softened. Add lemon rind, lemon juice and black pepper to taste; beat until well mixed. Turn the flavoured butter out on to a piece of clear film and shape into a log. Wrap in the clear film, then chill in the refrigerator for at least 1 hour before serving.

Cut into slices and serve on top of cooked fresh vegetables such as green beans, baby courgettes or baby sweetcorn. Flavoured butters are also ideal for serving on top of grilled meats, poultry, fish or shellfish. They are delicious served with hot toast or warm fresh bread.

Serves 4-6

LIME BUTTER: use the finely grated rind of 1 lime and lime juice in place of lemon rind and juice.

HERB BUTTER: omit the lemon rind and juice and beat 2 tablespoons chopped fresh mixed herbs such as parsley, chives and tarragon, into the softened butter with a squeeze of lemon juice.

GARLIC BUTTER: omit the lemon rind and beat 2 crushed cloves garlic and 2-3 teaspoons chopped fresh chives or parsley into the softened butter with the 2 teaspoons lemon juice.

ROAST TOMATO SAUCE

900g (2lb) cherry or baby plum tomatoes
1 tablespoon olive oil
1 red onion, finely chopped
2 cloves garlic, crushed
2 tablespoons sun-dried tomato purée
1 tablespoon chopped fresh oregano
salt and freshly ground black pepper

Preheat the oven to 180C (350F/Gas 4). Arrange the tomatoes in a single layer in a shallow ovenproof dish. Roast for 20 minutes or until soft. Remove from the oven and set aside to cool slightly, then purée in a blender or food processor until smooth.

Press the tomato purée through a sieve and discard the skins and seeds. Reserve the tomato sauce. Heat the oil in a saucepan, add the onion and garlic and sauté for 6-8 minutes, or until softened. Add reserved tomato sauce, tomato purée, chopped oregano and salt and pepper and mix well. (If you prefer a smoother sauce, simply process all the ingredients in a small blender or food processor until thoroughly combined.)

Bring to the boil, then reduce the heat and simmer, uncovered, for 10 minutes, stirring occasionally. Adjust the seasoning and serve with cooked vegetables such as cauliflower or broccoli florets, boiled new potatoes or roast vegetables. This sauce is also good served with grilled or baked chicken or fish.

Makes about 600ml (21fl oz/2¾ cups)
Serves 4-6

VARIATION: Use 2-3 tablespoons chopped fresh basil in place of oregano.

PINEAPPLE SALSA

300g (10oz) prepared fresh pineapple
6 spring onions
½ small yellow pepper, seeded
2 teaspoons finely grated peeled fresh root ginger
1 tablespoon freshly squeezed orange juice
1 tablespoon olive oil
1 teaspoon runny honey
1 tablespoon chopped fresh coriander
freshly ground black pepper

Finely chop the pineapple and place it in a bowl. Chop the spring onions and finely chop the yellow pepper. Add to the pineapple and stir to mix.

Put the ginger, orange juice, olive oil, honey and chopped coriander in a separate small bowl and mix well. Pour the orange juice mixture over the chopped vegetables and pineapple and toss to mix well.

Season to taste with black pepper. Cover and leave to stand at room temperature for about 30 minutes before serving. Serve with grilled or barbecued meat and poultry such as pork kebabs or chicken portions.

Serves 6

VARIATIONS: Use canned (drained) pineapple in place of fresh pineapple. Use red pepper in place of yellow pepper.

RED ONION SALSA

3 tomatoes
½ small red pepper, seeded
1 red onion
2 tablespoons tomato juice
1 tablespoon olive oil
2 teaspoons hot horseradish sauce
1 tablespoon chopped fresh flat-leaf parsley
salt and freshly ground black pepper

Using a sharp knife, cut a small cross in base of each tomato. Place the tomatoes in a bowl, cover with boiling water and leave for about 30 seconds or until the skins split.

Remove using a slotted spoon and plunge into cold water, then drain well. Peel off the skins, then halve the tomatoes and remove and discard the seeds. Finely chop the flesh and place it in a bowl. Finely chop the red pepper and onion and add to the chopped tomato. Put the tomato juice, olive oil, horseradish sauce and chopped parsley in a separate small bowl and mix well.

Add the tomato juice mixture to the chopped vegetables and toss to mix well. Season to taste with salt and pepper. Cover and leave to stand at room temperature for about 1 hour, to allow the flavours to develop. Serve with grilled, pan-fried or roast meats such as beef or lamb steaks. This salsa is also good served with grilled or baked fish such as salmon.

Serves 4-6

— MANGO & CORIANDER SALSA —

2 ripe mangoes
50g (2oz) cucumber
4 spring onions
1 tablespoon lime juice
3 tablespoons chopped fresh coriander
freshly ground black pepper

Peel, stone and finely chop the mangoes. Put the mango flesh in a bowl.

Finely chop the cucumber and spring onions and add to the mango flesh. Stir to mix.

Add the lime juice and chopped coriander and mix well. Season to taste with black pepper. Cover and leave to stand at room temperature for about 1 hour before serving. Serve with pan-fried or oven-baked chicken or turkey portions.

Serves 4-6

VARIATIONS: Use lemon juice in place of lime juice. Use chopped fresh mint in place of coriander.

FRESH TOMATO & CHILLI SAUCE

450g (1lb) plum tomatoes
2 shallots
1 fresh red or green chilli, cored and seeded
1 clove garlic, crushed
2 sun-dried tomatoes in oil, drained and
  finely chopped
1 tablespoon olive oil
1 tablespoon chopped fresh oregano
salt and freshly ground black pepper

Using a sharp knife, cut a small cross in base of each tomato. Place the tomatoes in a bowl, cover with boiling water and leave for about 30 seconds or until the skins split.

Remove using a slotted spoon and plunge into cold water, then drain well. Peel off the skins, then halve the tomatoes and remove and discard the seeds. Finely chop the flesh and place it in a bowl. Finely chop the shallots and chilli. Add to the chopped tomatoes and stir to mix.

Add the garlic, sun-dried tomatoes, olive oil and oregano, and mix well. Season with salt and pepper. Cover and leave to stand at room temperature for about 1 hour, before serving. Serve with grilled or baked fish such as red mullet, tuna or salmon, or with chargrilled chicken.

Serves 4

VARIATIONS: Use chopped fresh basil or coriander in place of oregano. Add a few drops of Tabasco sauce if liked.

SPICED PEACH SALSA

3 ripe peaches
4 spring onions
½ small yellow pepper, seeded
1 small fresh green chilli, cored and seeded
juice of ½ lime
2 teaspoons medium-hot chilli sauce
1 tablespoon chopped fresh coriander
1 tablespoon chopped fresh mint
freshly ground black pepper

Peel, stone and finely chop the peaches and place the chopped flesh in a bowl.

Finely chop the spring onions and yellow pepper and add to the chopped peach. Finely chop the chilli. Add the chilli to the peach flesh and stir to mix well.

Add the lime juice, chilli sauce and chopped herbs and mix well. Season to taste with black pepper. Cover and leave to stand at room temperature for at least 1 hour before serving. Serve with chargrilled tuna or salmon steaks or barbecued chicken or turkey portions. This salsa is also good served with cold cooked meats.

Serves 4-6

VARIATIONS: Use ripe nectarines in place of peaches.

— TOMATO & GARLIC RELISH —

2-3 beef tomatoes (total weight about 600g/1lb 5oz)
2 tablespoons olive oil
1 teaspoon cumin seeds (optional)
1 small red onion, finely chopped
2 cloves garlic, crushed
2 teaspoons balsamic vinegar
1 teaspoon light soft brown sugar
2 tablespoons chopped fresh basil
salt and freshly ground black pepper

Preheat the grill to high. Cut the tomatoes in half and place them, cut-side down, on a foil-lined rack in a grill pan. Grill the tomatoes until the skin is blistered and loose.

Remove from the grill, cool slightly, then peel off and discard the skins. Remove or squeeze out and discard the seeds. Chop the flesh and set aside. Heat the oil in a small saucepan, add the cumin seeds, if using, and cook for 30 seconds, stirring. Add the onion and garlic and sauté for 1-2 minutes. Add the tomato flesh and sauté gently for 4-5 minutes. If the tomatoes are especially juicy, sauté them over a high heat for a further 1-2 minutes, to reduce excess juice.

Remove the pan from the heat and stir in the balsamic vinegar, sugar and chopped basil, mixing well. Season to taste with salt and pepper. Serve warm with grilled or barbecued lamb, beef, chicken or tuna, or cold cooked meats.

Serves 4-6

VARIATIONS: Use 600g (1lb 5oz) plum or standard tomatoes, cut in half, in place of beef tomatoes. Use 2-3 shallots in place of red onion.

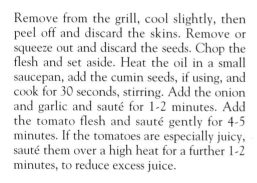
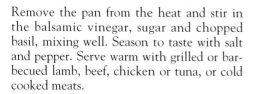

TROPICAL FRUIT RELISH

225g (8oz) prepared fresh pineapple, finely chopped
1 ripe nectarine or peach, peeled, stoned and finely
  chopped
1 ripe papaya, peeled, seeded and finely chopped
1 small yellow pepper, seeded and finely chopped
1 tablespoon runny honey
1 tablespoon lime juice
2 tablespoons chopped fresh coriander
freshly ground black pepper

Place the pineapple flesh in a bowl and add the chopped nectarine or peach and chopped papaya.

Add the yellow pepper to the bowl and stir to mix well. In a separate small bowl, mix the honey and lime juice together. Drizzle over the chopped fruit.

Add chopped coriander and toss to mix well. Season to taste with black pepper. Cover and leave to stand at room temperature for 30 minutes before serving. Serve with grilled fish such as monkfish, salmon or swordfish, or chargrilled chicken or turkey portions. This relish is also good served with hot or cold baked gammon.

Serves 6

VARIATION: Use ripe mango in place of pineapple.

SUMMER CORN RELISH

4 spring onions
8 red radishes
1 small red pepper
200g (7oz) can sweetcorn kernels, drained
1 tablespoon olive oil
2 teaspoons lemon juice
1 teaspoon Dijon mustard
2-3 tablespoons snipped fresh chives
salt and freshly ground black pepper

Chop the spring onions and finely chop the radishes. Seed and finely chop the red pepper.

Place the chopped spring onions, radishes and red pepper in a bowl. Add the sweetcorn kernels and stir to mix. In a separate small bowl, mix together the olive oil, lemon juice, mustard, chives and salt and pepper.

Pour over the sweetcorn mixture and toss well to mix. Cover and leave to stand at room temperature for about 30 minutes, before serving. Serve with grilled or barbecued chicken or turkey portions or kebabs.

Serves 4-6

VARIATIONS: Use 1 small red onion in place of spring onions. Use chopped fresh parsley or coriander in place of chives.

PEPPER, TOMATO & OLIVE RELISH

2 red peppers
1 yellow pepper
3 shallots, sliced
3 plum tomatoes, skinned, seeded and chopped
1 clove garlic, crushed
50g (2oz) pitted black olives, finely chopped
1 tablespoon olive oil (optional)
1 tablespoon chopped fresh basil
1 tablespoon chopped fresh flat-leaf parsley
salt and freshly ground black pepper

Preheat the grill to high. Cut the peppers in half and place them cut-side down on the rack in a grill pan.

Grill the peppers for 10-15 minutes until the skin is blackened and charred. Remove from the grill and cover the peppers with a clean damp tea towel. Set aside to cool. Meanwhile, place the shallot slices on the rack in the grill pan. Grill for about 5 minutes, turning once, until slightly softened. Remove from the grill and cool slightly. Remove the skin, cores and seeds from the peppers and chop the flesh. Finely chop the shallots. Place the chopped pepper flesh, shallots, tomatoes, garlic and olives in a bowl and stir to mix well.

Add the olive oil, if using, and chopped herbs and mix well. Season to taste with salt and pepper. Cover and set aside for about 1 hour before serving. Serve with grilled or pan-fried meat or poultry such as beef, pork or chicken, or grilled fish such as lemon sole or plaice.

Serves 4-6

VARIATIONS: Use standard tomatoes in place of plum tomatoes. Use chopped fresh oregano or marjoram in place of basil.

SALSA VERDE

1 small onion
2 cloves garlic
4 tablespoons chopped fresh parsley
2 tablespoons chopped fresh mint
1 tablespoon snipped fresh chives
1 tablespoon capers, drained and chopped
4 tablespoons olive oil
2 tablespoons lemon juice
1 teaspoon Dijon mustard
few drops of Tabasco sauce, or to taste
salt and freshly ground black pepper

Peel and finely chop the onion. Peel and crush the garlic cloves.

Place the onion, garlic, chopped herbs and capers in a small bowl and stir to mix. Add the olive oil, lemon juice and mustard and mix well. Add the Tabasco sauce and salt and pepper to taste.

Cover and leave to stand at room temperature for about 30 minutes, to allow the flavours to develop. Serve with grilled meats such as lamb, pork or beef steaks, or grilled fish such as haddock or monkfish.

Serves 4

VARIATIONS: Use lime juice in place of lemon juice. Omit the Tabasco sauce and add 1 finely chopped seeded fresh red or green chilli to the salsa. Peel, stone and finely chop 1 small avocado and add to the salsa, if liked.

ORIENTAL MARINADE

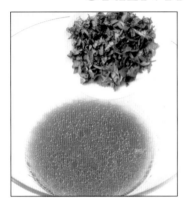

4 tablespoons orange juice
1 tablespoon olive oil
1 tablespoon dry sherry
1 tablespoon light soy sauce
1 tablespoon runny honey
2 tablespoons chopped fresh coriander
2 teaspoons finely grated peeled fresh root ginger
1 clove garlic, crushed
freshly ground black pepper

Put the orange juice, olive oil, sherry, soy sauce, honey, chopped coriander, ginger, garlic and black pepper in a non-metallic bowl or dish and mix together thoroughly.

Add poultry or meat to the marinade and turn to coat. Cover and leave to marinate in the refrigerator for 2-3 hours. If using fish, add to the marinade, turn to coat all over, then marinate for about 1 hour before cooking.

Remove the meat or fish from the marinade, reserving the marinade. Grill or barbecue the meat or fish until cooked, turning frequently and basting with the marinade during cooking, if liked. This marinade is enough to marinate about 450-700g (1-1½lb) poultry such as chicken or duck breast fillets, meat such as lamb cutlets, diced pork or beef steaks or fish such as monkfish, salmon or seafood.

Makes about 150ml (5fl oz/⅔ cup)
Serves 4-6

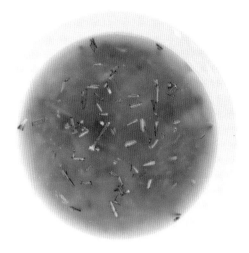

ROSEMARY & LEMON MARINADE

6 tablespoons olive oil
finely grated rind of 1 lemon
juice of 2 lemons
2 tablespoons finely chopped fresh rosemary
salt and freshly ground black pepper

Put the olive oil, lemon rind and juice, chopped rosemary and salt and pepper in a non-metallic bowl or dish and mix together thoroughly.

Add poultry or meat to the marinade and turn to coat. Cover and leave to marinate in the refrigerator for 2-3 hours. If using fish, add to the marinade, turn to coat all over, then marinate for about 1 hour before cooking. Remove the meat or fish from the marinade, reserving the marinade.

Grill or barbecue the meat or fish until cooked, turning frequently and basting with the marinade during cooking, if liked. This is enough to marinate about 450-700g (1-1½lb) poultry such as chicken or turkey breast fillets, meat such as lamb cutlets, lamb or beef steaks or kebabs or fish such as monkfish, cod or haddock. It is also ideal for marinating vegetables.

Makes about 200ml (7fl oz/1 cup)
Serves 4-6

MUSTARD MARINADE

4 tablespoons dry white wine
1 tablespoon olive oil
juice of ½ lemon
1 tablespoon wholegrain mustard
1 tablespoon Dijon mustard
salt and freshly ground black pepper

Put the wine, olive oil, lemon juice, mustards and salt and pepper in a non-metallic bowl or dish and mix together thoroughly.

Add poultry or meat to the marinade and turn to coat in the marinade. Cover and leave to marinate in the refrigerator for 2-3 hours. Remove the poultry or meat from the marinade, reserving the marinade. Grill or barbecue the poultry or meat until cooked, turning frequently and basting with the marinade during cooking, if liked.

This marinade is enough to marinate about 450-700g (1-1½lb) poultry such as chicken or turkey breast fillets or meat such as lamb, pork or beef steaks. It is also ideal for marinating chicken, meat or vegetable kebabs.

Makes about 175ml (6fl oz/¾ cup)
Serves 4-6

VARIATIONS: Use red wine or beer in place of white wine. Use juice of 1 lime in place of lemon juice.

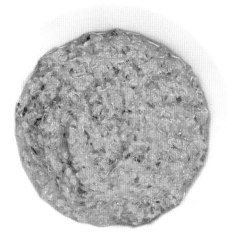

TANDOORI PASTE

1 red onion, cut into quarters
2 cloves garlic, peeled and roughly chopped
2.5cm (1in) piece fresh root ginger, peeled and
   roughly chopped
1 fresh red or green chilli, cored, seeded and chopped
juice of ½ lemon
1 tablespoon ground coriander
1 tablespoon ground cumin
2 teaspoons garam masala
1 teaspoon turmeric
1 teaspoon ground cinnamon
1 teaspoon olive oil
½ teaspoon each salt and freshly ground black pepper
2 tablespoons chopped fresh coriander
200ml (7fl oz/scant 1 cup) plain yogurt

Put the onion, garlic, ginger, chilli and
lemon juice in a small blender or food
processor and blend until finely chopped
(see above). Add all the ground spices, the
olive oil, salt and pepper and process to
form a relatively smooth paste. Transfer the
spice paste into a non-metallic bowl or dish,
add the chopped coriander and yogurt and
mix well.

Add poultry or meat to the paste and turn to
coat completely. Cover and marinate in the
refrigerator for at least 4 hours, or overnight.
Remove the poultry from the marinade.
Discard leftover paste. Grill or barbecue
poultry or meat until cooked, turning frequently and basting with melted ghee or oil
during cooking, if liked. This paste is enough
to marinate about 700-900g (1½-2lb)
chicken or turkey portions or breast fillets.

Makes about 450ml (16fl oz/2 cups)
Serves 6-8

TASTY BARBECUE PASTE

1 small onion
1 clove garlic
1 fresh red or green chilli
2 tablespoons tomato purée
1 tablespoon olive oil
2 teaspoons red wine vinegar
2 teaspoons light soft brown sugar
1 teaspoon Worcestershire sauce
1 teaspoon Dijon mustard
few drops of Tabasco sauce
salt and freshly ground black pepper

Peel and chop the onion. Peel and crush the garlic clove and seed and chop the chilli.

Put the onion, garlic and chilli in a small blender or food processor and process until finely chopped. Add the tomato purée, olive oil, vinegar, sugar, Worcestershire sauce, mustard, Tabasco sauce and salt and pepper and process to mix well. Transfer the barbecue paste into a non-metallic bowl or dish. Add the poultry or meat to the paste and turn to coat lightly. Alternatively, brush or spread the paste over the meat. Cover and marinate in the refrigerator for at least 4 hours, or overnight.

Remove the poultry or meat from the barbecue paste and scrape off most of the paste before cooking. Discard leftover paste. Grill or barbecue the poultry or meat until cooked, turning frequently and brushing lightly with oil during cooking, if liked. This paste is enough to marinate about 450g (1lb) poultry such as chicken or turkey portions or breast fillets or meat such as beef steaks or lamb chops.

Makes about 175ml (6fl oz/¾ cup)
Serves 4

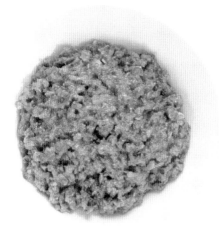

MOROCCAN PASTE

3 shallots
2 cloves garlic
2 tablespoons olive oil
2 tablespoons lime juice
1 teaspoon ground cumin
1 teaspoon ground coriander
1 teaspoon hot chilli powder
½ teaspoon turmeric
¼ teaspoon ground cinnamon
2 tablespoons chopped fresh coriander
salt and freshly ground black pepper

Roughly chop shallots. Crush garlic cloves. Put in a small blender or food processor and process until finely chopped.

Add the olive oil, lime juice, ground spices, chopped coriander and salt and pepper and process until thoroughly mixed to form a paste. Transfer the paste into a non-metallic bowl or dish. Add the meat or poultry to the paste and turn to coat lightly. Alternatively, brush or spread the paste over the meat. Cover and marinate in the refrigerator for at least 4 hours, or overnight. Remove the meat or poultry from the paste and scrape off most of the paste before cooking. Discard leftover paste.

Grill or barbecue the meat or poultry until cooked, turning frequently and brushing lightly with oil during cooking, if liked. This paste is enough to coat and marinate about 450g (1lb) meat such as lamb or beef kebabs or steaks or poultry such as chicken, turkey or duck portions or breast fillets.

Makes about 150ml (5fl oz/⅔ cup)
Serves 4

VARIATION: Use lemon juice in place of lime juice.

— LIME & GINGER MARINADE —

3 tablespoons olive oil
1 teaspoon sesame oil (optional)
finely grated rind of 1 lime
juice of 2 limes
4cm (1½in) piece fresh root ginger, peeled and finely
  grated
1 clove garlic, crushed
salt and freshly ground black pepper

Put the olive oil, sesame oil, if using, lime
rind and juice, ginger, garlic and salt and
pepper in a non-metallic bowl or dish and
mix together thoroughly.

Add poultry or meat to the marinade and
turn to coat. Cover and leave to marinate in
the refrigerator for 2-3 hours. If using fish,
add to the marinade, turn to coat all over,
then marinate for about 1 hour before
cooking. Remove the poultry, meat or fish
from the marinade, reserving the marinade.

Grill or barbecue the poultry, meat or fish
until cooked, turning frequently and basting
with the marinade during cooking, if liked.
This marinade is enough to marinate about
450-700g (1-1½lb) poultry such as chicken
or turkey breast fillets, meat such as lamb
cutlets, pork chops or beef steaks or white
fish fillets such as cod, haddock or plaice. It
is also ideal for marinating chicken or meat
kebabs.

Makes about 150ml (5fl oz/⅔ cup)
Serves 4-6

CRÈME ANGLAISE

300ml (10fl oz/1¼ cups) milk
1 vanilla pod, split in half lengthways
3 egg yolks
1 tablespoon caster sugar

Pour the milk into a small heavy-based saucepan, add the vanilla pod and heat gently until almost boiling. Remove the pan from the heat and set aside to infuse for 15 minutes. Remove and discard the vanilla pod. Put the egg yolks and sugar in a bowl and whisk together until thick and creamy.

Gradually whisk in the hot infused milk, then strain back into the saucepan. Cook over a low heat, stirring continuously, for about 10 minutes, or until the mixture thickens enough to thinly coat the back of a wooden spoon. Do not allow the mixture to boil or it may curdle. Serve hot or cold.

If serving cold, pour the egg custard into a clean bowl and cover the surface closely with a piece of non-stick baking paper, to prevent a skin forming, and allow to cool. Serve with grilled, baked or stewed fruit, hot baked or steamed fruit puddings or fruit crumbles.

Makes about 350ml (12fl oz/1½ cups)
Serves 4

VARIATION: Infuse the milk with the pared rind of 1 lemon in place of vanilla pod.

— BASIC SWEET WHITE SAUCE —

5 teaspoons cornflour
300ml (10fl oz/1¼ cups) milk
knob of butter
5 teaspoons caster sugar, or to taste

Put the cornflour in a small bowl, add a little of the milk and mix together until smooth. Heat the remaining milk in a small saucepan with the butter, until just boiling. Pour the hot milk on to the cornflour mixture, stirring continuously. Return the mixture to the saucepan and bring slowly to the boil, stirring, until the sauce thickens.

Simmer gently for 2-3 minutes, stirring. Stir in the sugar to taste. Serve hot with fruit puddings, pies and tarts.

Makes about 300ml (10fl oz/1¼ cups)
Serves 4

LEMON/ORANGE SAUCE
Follow the recipe for Basic Sweet White Sauce. Stir in the finely grated rind of 1 lemon or 1 small orange just before serving.

QUICK VANILLA SAUCE
Follow the recipe for Basic Sweet White Sauce. Stir in ½-1 teaspoon vanilla essence, or to taste, just before serving.

QUICK CHOCOLATE SAUCE
Blend 3-4 teaspoons cocoa powder with 2 tablespoons of hot water until smooth, then set aside. Follow the recipe for Basic Sweet White Sauce. Once the sauce has thickened, stir in the cocoa paste and reheat gently until hot, stirring. Stir in sugar to taste and serve.

NECTARINE COULIS

4 ripe nectarines
2 tablespoons fresh orange juice
25g (1oz/5 teaspoons) caster sugar, or to taste
2-3 teaspoons brandy, or to taste (optional)

Peel, halve and stone the nectarines and roughly chop the flesh. Put nectarine flesh in a saucepan with orange juice and sugar. Heat gently, stirring, until sugar has dissolved. Bring slowly to the boil, then cover and simmer for 10-15 minutes or until the fruit is soft, stirring occasionally. Remove the pan from the heat and cool slightly.

Mash the fruit, then press the mixture through a nylon sieve into a bowl. Discard the contents of the sieve.

Stir the brandy, if using, into the nectarine coulis, then taste for sweetness and stir in more sugar, if necessary. Serve warm or cold with prepared fresh fruit such as strawberries or raspberries, crêpes or pancakes, iced desserts or ice cream.

Makes about 300ml (10fl oz/1¼ cups)
Serves 4-6

VARIATIONS: Use rum or orange-flavoured liqueur such as Cointreau in place of brandy.

— CHOCOLATE FUDGE SAUCE —

175g (6oz) good quality plain chocolate
100ml (3½ fl oz/scant ½ cup) double cream
50g (2oz/⅓ cup) light soft brown sugar
50g (2oz/2 tablespoons) golden syrup
15g (½oz/1 tablespoon) butter

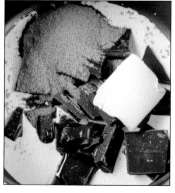

Break the chocolate into squares. Place the chocolate, cream, sugar, golden syrup and butter in a small heavy-based saucepan.

Heat gently, stirring, until the chocolate has melted and the sugar has dissolved. Bring slowly to the boil, stirring, then simmer very gently for 1-2 minutes, stirring occasionally.

Cool slightly before serving, then serve hot or warm with grilled or baked fruit, hot vanilla or chocolate sponge puddings or desserts, profiteroles or ice cream.

Makes about 325ml (11fl oz/1⅓ cups)
Serves 4-6

— WHITE CHOCOLATE SAUCE —

175g (6oz) white chocolate
150ml (5fl oz/²⁄₃ cup) double cream
15g (½oz/1 tablespoon) butter

Roughly chop the chocolate.

Put the chocolate, cream and butter into a heatproof bowl. Place the bowl over a pan of simmering water.

Heat gently, stirring, until the ingredients have melted together and the sauce is well blended and smooth. Serve warm or at room temperature with raw or grilled fruit, hot sponge or baked puddings or fruit tarts. If serving the sauce cold, stir it well before serving.

Makes about 300ml (10fl oz/1¼ cups)
Serves 4-6

VARIATION: Use milk chocolate in place of white chocolate.

— BUTTERSCOTCH NUT SAUCE —

85g (3oz/¾ cup) chopped walnuts
40g (1½oz/3 tablespoons) butter
115g (4oz/¼ cup) caster sugar
1 tablespoon lemon juice
200ml (7fl oz/scant 1 cup) double cream

Spread the walnuts out in a grill pan then toast under the grill for 2-3 minutes, turning frequently until lightly browned. Set aside to cool.

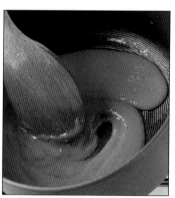

Put the butter in a small heavy-based pan and heat gently until melted. Add the sugar and cook, stirring, to a dark caramel. Remove from the heat and stir in 5 tablespoons hot water and the lemon juice. Take care when adding the water as the mixture may spit.

Return the pan to the heat and stir until smooth. Add the cream then cook gently, stirring, for 1-2 minutes to make a smooth sauce. Remove from the heat and stir in the walnuts. Serve with roast apples or pears, ice cream or steamed puddings.

Makes about 425ml (15fl oz/2 cups)
Serves 6-8

BLACK CHERRY SAUCE

225g (8oz) pitted black or dark red cherries
½ cinnamon stick
50g (2oz/¼ cup) caster sugar, or to taste
2-3 teaspoons kirsch, or to taste
1 teaspoon cornflour or arrowroot

Put the cherries and cinnamon stick in a small heavy-based saucepan with 100ml (3½fl oz/scant ½ cup) water. Cover, bring slowly to the boil, then simmer gently, stirring occasionally, until the cherries are softened. Remove and discard the cinnamon stick.

Add sugar to taste, stirring until dissolved, then add the kirsch to taste. In a small bowl, blend the cornflour or arrowroot with 1 tablespoon cold water, then stir the cornflour or arrowroot mixture into the cherry sauce. (Add ½-1 teaspoon extra cornflour or arrowroot if you prefer a slightly thicker sauce.)

Bring slowly to the boil, stirring, until the sauce thickens. Simmer gently for 2-3 minutes, stirring. Serve hot with steamed or baked sponge or chocolate puddings, pancakes, crêpes or ice cream.

Makes about 300ml (10fl oz/1¼ cups)
Serves 4

VARIATIONS: Use brandy in place of kirsch. Use light soft brown sugar in place of caster sugar.

TANGY LEMON SAUCE

150ml (5fl oz/⅔ cup) double cream
150g (5oz/⅔ cup) plain fromage frais (8% fat)
4 tablespoons luxury lemon curd
finely grated rind of 1 small lemon (optional)

Put the cream and fromage frais into a bowl and whip together until the mixture thickens and just holds its shape.

Fold in the lemon curd and lemon rind, if using, until well combined.

Serve with fresh fruit such as sliced strawberries or peaches, fresh fruit salad or cold fruit tarts.

Serves 6-8

VARIATIONS: Use the finely grated rind of 1 lime and lime curd in place of lemon rind and lemon curd. Fold the lemon curd and lemon rind into 300ml (10fl oz/1¼ cups) un-whipped crème fraîche, if liked.

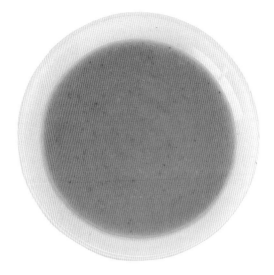

STRAWBERRY-RHUBARB SAUCE

225g (8oz/1⅔ cups) strawberries
225g (8oz) rhubarb, trimmed
50g (2oz/¼ cup) butter
50g (2oz/¼ cup) caster sugar, or to taste
1 tablespoon amaretto

Hull and halve the strawberries. Cut the rhubarb into 1cm (½in) pieces.

Put the strawberries and rhubarb into a saucepan with the butter and 100ml (3½fl oz/scant ½ cup) water. Heat gently, stirring occasionally, until the mixture comes to the boil, then cover and simmer for about 10 minutes, until the rhubarb is soft. Remove the pan from the heat and cool slightly, then purée the mixture in a blender or food processor until smooth. Return the mixture to the rinsed-out pan.

Stir in sugar to taste, then reheat gently, stirring, until the sugar has dissolved. Bring slowly to the boil, stirring occasionally, then stir in the amaretto. Serve hot or cold with fruit pies, hot baked or sponge puddings, pancakes, creamy desserts or ice cream.

Makes about 550ml (20fl oz/2½ cups)
Serves 6

VARIATIONS: Use raspberries in place of strawberries. Use light soft brown sugar in place of caster sugar.

MOCHA CUSTARD

4 teaspoons custard powder
1 tablespoon light soft brown sugar
300ml (10fl oz/1¼ cups) milk
1-2 teaspoons instant coffee granules, or to taste
50g (2oz) plain chocolate, broken into squares
few drops of vanilla essence (optional)

Put the custard powder in a small bowl with the sugar. Add a little of the milk and mix to form a smooth paste. Set aside. In a separate small bowl, dissolve the coffee granules in 1 tablespoon hot water.

Add the dissolved coffee to the custard paste and mix well. Set aside. Put the remaining milk in a small heavy-based saucepan, add the chocolate and heat gently until the chocolate has melted, stirring occasionally. Pour the hot chocolate milk on to the blended custard mixture, stirring continuously.

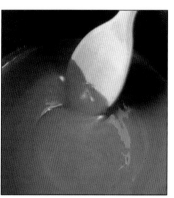

Return the mixture to the pan and heat gently, stirring continuously, until the custard sauce comes to the boil and thickens. Simmer gently for 1-2 minutes, stirring. Stir in the vanilla essence, if using. Serve hot with hot baked or steamed sponge puddings or upside-down fruit puddings.

Makes about 325ml (11fl oz/1⅓ cups)
Serves 4

VARIATION: Use 1 tablespoon caster sugar in place of soft brown sugar.

MELBA SAUCE

4 tablespoons redcurrant jelly
225g (8oz) raspberries
25g (1oz/2 tablespoons) icing sugar, sifted
1 tablespoon framboise liqueur or kirsch, or to taste

Put the redcurrant jelly in a small saucepan and heat gently until melted. Remove the pan from the heat.

Put the raspberries in a small blender or food processor. Add the melted redcurrant jelly, icing sugar and framboise liqueur or kirsch and blend to form a smooth purée.

Press the purée though a nylon sieve and discard the contents of the sieve. Pour the sauce into a jug and serve with poached pears or peaches, meringues or ice cream.

Makes about 225ml (8fl oz/1 cup)
Serves 4

VARIATION: Use blackberries, loganberries or tayberries in place of raspberries.

MARMALADE SAUCE

1 orange
5 tablespoons orange marmalade
2 teaspoons arrowroot
1-2 teaspoons brandy (optional)

Squeeze the juice from the orange. Pour the juice into a measuring jug and make up to 150ml (5fl oz/⅔ cup) with cold water. Pour the mixed orange juice and water into a small saucepan.

Add the marmalade and stir to mix. Heat gently, stirring occasionally, until the marmalade has dissolved, then bring the mixture gently to the boil. In a small bowl, blend the arrowroot with 1 tablespoon of cold water. Pour the hot marmalade mixture on to the arrowroot mixture, stirring continuously. Return the mixture to the saucepan and bring slowly to the boil, stirring, until the sauce thickens.

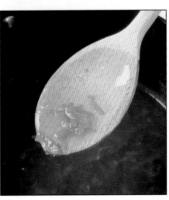

Simmer gently for 1-2 minutes, stirring, then stir in the brandy, if using. Serve hot with steamed or baked sponge puddings, fruit puddings or ice cream.

Makes about 200ml (7fl oz/1 cup)
Serves 4

VARIATION: Use juice of 1 lemon and 1 lime and lemon and lime marmalade in place of orange juice and orange marmalade and omit the brandy.

ORANGE & GINGER SAUCE

1 orange
4 pieces of preserved stem ginger in syrup, drained
 (about 50g/2oz total weight)
2 teaspoons arrowroot
25g (1oz/2 tablespoons) light soft brown sugar
1 tablespoon ginger syrup from the jar of preserved
 stem ginger

Finely grate the rind from the orange and squeeze the juice. Finely chop the stem ginger. Set aside.

In a small bowl, blend the arrowroot with 1 tablespoon cold water. Set aside. Put the orange juice in a small heavy-based saucepan with the sugar and 100ml (3½fl oz/scant ½ cup) water. Heat gently, stirring, until the sugar has dissolved, then bring to the boil. Pour the hot orange liquid on to the arrowroot mixture, stirring continuously.

Return the mixture to the saucepan and stir in the ginger syrup, orange rind and chopped ginger. Bring slowly to the boil, stirring, until the sauce thickens, then simmer gently for 1-2 minutes, stirring. Serve hot with steamed or baked puddings or fresh or dried fruit salads or compotes.

Makes about 225ml (8fl oz/1 cup)
Serves 4

VARIATION: Use caster sugar in place of soft brown sugar.

RUM & RAISIN SAUCE

50g (2oz/⅓ cup) raisins
1 tablespoon cornflour
200ml (7fl oz/scant 1 cup) milk
100ml (3½fl oz/scant ½ cup) double cream
15g (½oz/1 tablespoon) butter
1 tablespoon light soft brown sugar
2 tablespoons rum

Roughly chop the raisins, then set aside. In a small bowl, blend the cornflour with 2 tablespoons of the milk until smooth. Set aside.

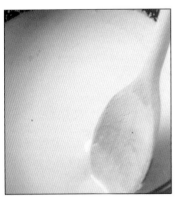

Heat the remaining milk, the cream and butter in a small heavy-based saucepan, until almost boiling. Pour the hot milk and cream mixture on to the cornflour mixture, stirring continuously. Return the mixture to the saucepan and bring slowly to the boil, stirring, until the sauce thickens. Simmer gently for 2-3 minutes, stirring.

Stir in the sugar, rum and chopped raisins and reheat gently until hot. Serve hot with pancakes, crêpes, sponge puddings or ice cream.

Makes about 375ml (13fl oz/1⅔ cups)
Serves 4

VARIATIONS: Use chopped ready-to-eat dried prunes, apricots, figs or sultanas in place of raisins. Use milk in place of double cream.

FOREST FRUIT COULIS

350g (12oz) mixed prepared fresh berries such as
  raspberries, strawberries, blackberries,
  blackcurrants and redcurrants
50g (2oz/¼ cup) caster sugar, or to taste
2-3 teaspoons crème de cassis, or to taste

Place the mixed berries in a saucepan with
the sugar and 2 tablespoons water. Heat
gently, stirring, until the sugar has dissolved.
Bring slowly to the boil, then cover the pan
and cook gently for 10-15 minutes, or until
the fruit is pulpy, stirring occasionally.

Remove the pan from the heat, cool
slightly, then press the pulp and juice
through a nylon sieve. Discard the contents
of the sieve.

Stir the crème de cassis into the fruit coulis,
then taste for sweetness and stir in more
sugar and crème de cassis, if necessary. Serve
warm or cold with fresh fruit tartlets, crêpes
or pancakes, yogurt ice or ice cream.

Makes about 300ml (10fl oz/1¼ cups)
Serves 4-6

VARIATION: Use other fruit-flavoured
liqueurs such as cherry or framboise liqueur
or sloe gin in place of crème de cassis.

RASPBERRY COULIS

225g (8oz/1⅔ cups) raspberries
15g (½oz/1 tablespoon) icing sugar, sifted, or to taste
2 teaspoons framboise liqueur or kirsch, or to taste
(optional)

Put the raspberries in a small blender or
food processor and blend to form a purée.

Press the raspberry purée through a nylon
sieve into a bowl to remove the seeds.
Discard the seeds.

Add icing sugar to the raspberry coulis to
taste, stirring to mix well. Stir in the framboise liqueur or kirsch, if using. Serve cold
with creamy cold desserts, fresh fruit, ice
creams, sorbets or yogurt ices.

Makes about 175ml (6fl oz/¾ cup)
Serves 4

VARIATIONS: Use blackberries or strawberries in place of raspberries and add icing
sugar and liqueur to taste. Use frozen
(defrosted) raspberries in place of fresh.

APRICOT & CINNAMON COULIS

400g (14oz) can apricot halves in juice
1 teaspoon ground cinnamon
25g (1oz/2 tablespoons) icing sugar, sifted
2 teaspoons amaretto (optional)

Put the apricots and their juice in a small blender or food processor and blend until smooth. Add the cinnamon and blend until well mixed.

Press the apricot purée through a nylon sieve into a bowl. Discard the contents of the sieve.

Whisk or fold the icing sugar into the apricot coulis until well mixed. Stir in the amaretto, if using. Serve with cold creamy desserts, fruit desserts or ice cream.

Makes about 275ml (9½fl oz/1¼ cups)
Serves 4-6

VARIATIONS: Use canned peaches in place of apricots. Use ¼-½ teaspoon almond extract or to taste, in place of amaretto, if liked.

INDEX